GROWING MAGIC MUSHROOMS MADE SIMPLE

A STEP BY STEP GUIDE ON GROWING MAGIC MUSHROOMS

JOEY FERELL

Table of Contents

CHAPTER ONE

HOW TO GROW MAGIC MUSHROOMS.

Creating Magic Mushrooms

Please tell me how to grow psilocybin mushrooms. You're not the only one. Because of these factors, more people appear to be interested in doing so.

- An increase in interest in magic mushroom's health benefits

- Possibility of cost savings

An increase in the availability of mushroom-growing guides and kits

- The shifting legal landscape: Magic mushrooms are gradually becoming legal in more and more U.S. cities.

For those of you who have decided to grow magic mushrooms, we've put together a detailed guide. Psilocybin mushrooms can be grown at home for a fraction of the cost, making it a worthwhile endeavor. Depending on your location, there may be legal ramifications to doing so.

Grow Magic Mushrooms at Home with these instructions.

Let's get into the nitty-gritty of growing magic mushrooms now. This guide is intended for those who are new to the mushroom-growing hobby.

There will be a finished product ready for consumption in 4-6 weeks, assuming everything goes according to plan.

Pick Your Favorite Mushroom

Determine the type of mushroom you'd like to grow before anything else. Magic mushroom spores—the reproductive cells that can grow into mushrooms—are only available for a limited number of species in nature. Varieties of individual species can also be purchased.

Choosing a strain or species that appeals to you is the most important step in determining how much to take.

Equipment and Ingredients

The ingredients and equipment you'll need to grow your own psilocybin mushrooms will vary. It's a one-time investment, but that's a good thing. You'll save a lot of money by making your own magic mushrooms rather than purchasing them from street vendors or darknet vendors.

Ingredients:

• 10-12 cc. Spore syringe Your psilocybin mushroom spores will be in this container. The spores are "sown" into the substrate using this device. (It's worth noting that some growers have reported problems with spore syringes, such as contamination, the wrong strain, or even nothing but water. The spore syringe should come from a trusted source.)

• Flour made from brown rice that is organic

Fine to medium-grained Vermiculite

• Consuming water

Equipment:

CHAPTER 2

A total of 12 half-pint jars
without shoulders and lids

• Small hammer and nail

• Cup for measuring

• Bowl for mixing

• Strainer

Heavy-duty tin foil.

Steaming in a large pot with a tight-fitting lid

• Towel of modest size

• Tape with micropores

• 50-115-liter clear plastic storage container

The drill bit should be a quarter of an inch in diameter.

- Perlite

Bottle with atomizing mist

sanitary products:

- Alcoholic swab

- Torch lighter with butane or propane fuel

- A disinfectant for the surface.

• Sanitizer for the air

• Surgical mask, sterile latex gloves, and a glove box (all optional)

Psilocybin Mushrooms: A Step-by-Step Guide

To begin, you'll need to do some prep work.

In each of the lids, make four evenly spaced holes with a hammer and a nail that have been disinfected with rubbing alcohol.

Each jar should contain two-thirds of a cup of vermiculite and one-quarter of a cup of water. Use a disinfected strainer to remove the extra liquid. A quarter cup of brown rice is added per half-pint jar of vermiculite to the bowl, which is then combined with the vermiculite.

• Fill the jars to within half an inch of the rims, but don't overfill them. Then, use rubbing alcohol to disinfect the top half-inch. Dry vermiculite should then be placed on top of your jars (this will insulate the substrate from contaminants).

• Screw the lids down firmly. Insulate the jars by wrapping them in foil. Keep the foil edges in place by securing them around the jars' perimeters. Water and condensation will not be able to enter the holes as a result of this. Next, place the jars on top of the small towel in your large cooking pot, making sure they don't touch the bottom of the pot. After that, fill the jars halfway with tap water and slowly bring them to a boil, watching to make sure they don't tip over. Finally, cover the pot with a tight-fitting lid and let it steam for 75-90 minutes, according to the recipe.

Leave the foil-covered jars in the pot to cool down for several hours or overnight after you've finished steaming. Before moving on, make sure they're at room temperature.

Inoculation is the next step.

• Heat the needle of your syringe with a lighter until it glows bright red. To avoid contamination, allow the needle to cool completely before wiping it down with alcohol. After that, shake the syringe by pulling back on the plunger (this will evenly distribute the psilocybin mushroom spores). You want to avoid contamination if you have to assemble the syringe before using it. Sterilized latex gloves and a surgical mask can be used to perform this procedure, and a disinfected still air container or glove box is ideal.

Using a syringe with a long enough needle, slowly inject the solution into the first jar. Inject a quarter-cc of the spore solution into the jar with the needle resting against the side of the jar. After each injection, wipe the needle with alcohol and repeat this procedure for the remaining three holes in the skin. After that, use micropore tape to seal up the holes and store the jar in a cool, dry place without the foil. For each of the remaining jars, sterilize the needle with the lighter and alcohol before each inoculation.

Colonization is the third and final step in the process.

Place the inoculated jars in an area that is clean, out of direct sunlight, and at a temperature that is comfortable for the bacteria. Between seven and 14 days after inoculation, white, fluffy-looking mycelium should begin to spread outward from the inoculation sites. This is a good time to look for any signs of contamination, such as odd colors or smells. You should get rid of the jars right away if you see any of these symptoms. It's always better to be safe than sorry if you're unsure about a product's safety.)

• The jars should be colonized after 3-4 weeks. Allow another seven days for the mycelium to firmly establish itself on the surface.

CHAPTER 3

A quarter-inch hole should be drilled into the container's sides, base, and lid at two-inch intervals. A block of wood should be drilled from inside out to ensure that the container does not crack during this step. Then, with the box on top, place four solid objects in the corners of the room to allow air to circulate beneath it. Covering the bottom of the box may also be helpful in protecting it from moisture leakage.

To soak the perlite, place it in a strainer and run cold water over it. Spread the perlite over the bottom of your grow chamber after allowing the water to drain until it stops dripping. If you want a thicker layer of perlite, keep going until you've covered the entire area with it.

It's time to eat!

In order to avoid damaging the substrates (or "cakes"), open the jars and remove the dry vermiculite layer from each one.

Then, remove the cakes from the jars by flipping them over and tapping them on a disinfected surface.

• Using a cold water faucet, rinse the cakes one at a time. Vermiculite will be flushed away in this manner. Place the cakes in the pot after filling it with warm water. To submerge them, you may want to use another pot or another heavy object, such as a frying pan. The next step is to let the pot sit at room temperature for up to 24 hours before using it. This will allow the cakes to rehydrate in sufficient time.

The cakes should be taken out of the water and then placed on a clean, disinfected surface. The next step is to add dry vermiculite to the mixing bowl. Next, one by one, roll each cake into the vermiculite, making sure it is completely covered.

Remove the perlite from the grow chamber by cutting out a tin foil square large enough to hold each cake. Place the cakes on top of the foil squares inside the chamber and mist the chamber with the spray bottle. Before securing the lid, give the chamber one last fanning with the lid open.

• At this point, you'll want to mist the chamber about four times a day to keep the humidity level stable. However, don't wet the cakes with water before baking them. After misting, you should also fan the chamber with the lid up to six times a day to help increase airflow. The mushrooms will grow if the mycelium is exposed to ambient light during the day.

Harvesting is the sixth and final step.

Be on the Lookout. They begin as tiny white bumps, and then grow into pin-like mushrooms (fruits). The mushrooms will be ready to be harvested in 5-12 days.

• When the cake is done baking, cut the mushrooms close to the cake. Psilocybin mushrooms lose potency as they mature, so don't wait until they're done growing.

It is legal to grow magic mushrooms in the United States.

Because magic mushroom spores do not contain psilocybin, they are generally legal to buy and possess. Psilocybin mushroom spores are legal in all but three states: California, Georgia, and Idaho. Legislators in these states are working to make it illegal to grow magic mushrooms.

Once the spores germinate, the resulting psilocybin mushrooms will be illegal outside of these three states because they contain psilocybin. As a result, you should be aware of the potential legal ramifications if you decide to grow your own.

THE END